75

HAUS CURIOSITIES

Brexit and the British

About the Author

Stephen Green was an international banker and Minister for Trade and Investment between 2011–3013. He chairs the Natural History Museum and Asia House, is an ordained priest of the Church of England and is a member of the House of Lords. He is the author of *The European Identity: Historical and Cultural Realities We Cannot Deny* and *Reluctant Meister: How Germany's Past is Shaping its European Future.*

Stephen Green

BREXIT AND THE BRITISH

Who Are We Now?

**HAUS
CURIOSITIES**

First published by Haus Publishing in 2017
70 Cadogan Place
London SW1X 9AH
www.hauspublishing.com

A CIP catalogue record for this book is
available from the British Library

ISBN: 978-1-910376-71-3
eISBN: 978-1-910376-72-0

Typeset in Garamond by MacGuru Ltd

Printed in Spain

Acknowledgements

My thoughts on what Brexit tells us about the British have been fermenting ever since the referendum result on 24 June, 2016. They have been moulded by conversations with many people, both in Britain and on the Continent. In particular, my thanks go to four people who commented carefully and thoughtfully on my essay in various drafts: Peter Hennessy, Martin Donnelly, Caroline MacDonald-Haig and Philip Welsh. All four brought a wealth of historical depth to the topic, providing both challenge and confirmation where appropriate. Their differing perspectives have helped me shape my views. The result is my own responsibility of course, but it is much the better for their support.

Contents

The shock and its aftermath

It feels like a long time now since I woke up very early on the morning after the Brexit vote in June 2016. My wife had made the mistake of looking at the news. She crept out of the bedroom to go downstairs, and in so doing she woke me up. I realised instantly that something had happened. So I looked at my phone and saw what she had seen. It was around 4 o'clock – still dark on one of the shortest nights of the year – and by then the result was clear. The news of the 52–48 result was a shock and sleep vanished instantly. I remember noting that at least it was a clear-cut result, even if it was not the one I had wanted or expected. I followed my wife downstairs, where we sat and watched the events unfold on the television. Much has happened since then; but still it is one of those moments – like a birth or a death in the family – that we will remember for the rest of our lives.

Over the following days, the mood amongst Remainers was a swirling mix of disbelief, dismay and anger. Even the Leavers seemed surprised. It became clear very quickly that few if any of the Leave campaigners had much idea of what Brexit would mean in specifics. Few people in either business or government had much idea either. The markets had clearly been assuming it would not happen – hence the very sharp fall in sterling, which had been driven up strongly in advance. The online betting market had made exactly the same mistake. I had gone to bed on the day of the vote thinking it would be close but that the Remainers had the edge: even the prominent Leavers interviewed on the television that evening seemed braced for a narrow loss.

For a while, some Remainers, who seemed to become more passionate in defeat than they had been at any stage in the campaign, pinned their hopes on an online petition for a new referendum. This gathered over four million signatures over the weekend – remarkable enough, but nowhere near what would have been needed to convince government or parliament of the need for a rerun or simply to ignore the result. The fact was that more people in Britain had voted to leave the EU than had ever voted for anything. A few went on hoping that it might not in the end come to an actual Brexit; that some new grand bargain, which in effect changed the nature of the EU, would allow continued participation in the European project on some basis more acceptable to the British people. More generally, though, there was little sign of 'buyer's remorse'. Some Leavers might have been nervous about whether they had done the right thing by their children (as one father of a nine-year-old confessed to me). But not many. Most people, Leavers and Remainers alike, began to get used to a new reality, even while they were unsure what final form it would take. And many were lulled by the unexpectedly robust performance of the economy in the months after the vote. The sky had not fallen in.

And then Article 50 was triggered; the government won a mandate for its Brexit strategy at the June general election – the phoney war was over. Some have continued to exude confidence and optimism because they believe that rational self-interest will ensure a good result from the negotiations – or because they are whistling in the dark. Some feel the energy of excitement; for them, Britain had now voted to enter a brave new world. Others are stoic but quietly nervous, kept awake at night by the sheer complexity of the task. And most have become reconciled to the thought that it could take years to sort out all the intricacies of a new relationship between Britain and the EU. Increasingly, the Remainers have focussed on the longer term: Britain will, they argue, find out that 'the gravitational pull of a unified Europe on our medium-sized nation is too strong'.* But the biggest question Britain has posed itself since the Second World War remains open: can the British find a reasonable modus vivendi with their European neighbours, at the same time as building new and exciting relationships in the wider world?

We shall see. Much of the campaigning before the vote had been a cacophony of exaggeration and lies, some of which rankled deeply and which badly wounded many relationships in the rest of the EU and indeed beyond.† In the last analysis,

---

* From an article by Janan Ganesh in the *Financial Times*, 20 February, 2017. This envisages the Remainers pushing for ever closer relationships with the European Union over the coming decade: for sector-by-sector opt-ins to the Single Market; for alignment with European state aid and environmental protection policies as they evolve; and for coordination of foreign and defence policies with Berlin and Paris. Ganesh argues, surely correctly, that much of this will, in fact, be inevitable in the British national interest.

† References to the spectre of Nazism were deeply hurtful to modern Germans, for example. And lies about Turkey joining the EU, prompting denials which implied that Turkey would never be fit to

the Remain campaign was hobbled throughout because no one could plausibly deny that the EU was (and is) in need of radical reform. This made any simple and straightforward defence of the status quo difficult.

And virtually nobody was prepared to argue that a European identity was a fundamental element in a modern British self-awareness, to be celebrated and valued as such. In fact, much of the debate was dominated purely by economic calculations: both sides argued at length in terms of the costs and benefits of membership of the EU relative to alternative trade strategies, and about the costs of disruption involved in leaving it. Projections were batted back and forth, often with spurious precision, as if anyone could plausibly quantify the difference between alternative visions of Britain's economic performance ten or twenty years ahead.

Yet those arguments were not what carried the day. The real debate was about the stranger in our midst. Londoners might be relaxed about – or even delight in – living in Babel, and the Remainers argued in terms of the economic benefits of immigration. The Leavers, on the other hand, found angry resonance when they conjured up the demons of uncontrolled immigration. All in all, one side appeared to lack much conviction; the other was full of passionate

---

join the EU, were deeply resented by modern Turks who have seen the UK as their friend – especially at a time when they feel under siege by a new leadership which is busy unravelling the secularist settlement on which their country was founded. One way and another, post-Brexit Britain has many bridges to rebuild, with countries that matter to it economically and/or geopolitically.

intensity. And this was a binary affair: there was no centre to hold.

Not much in all this did justice to the complexity of the case for or against membership of the EU – a case which was inevitably multilayered. It involved questions about sovereignty: can it be shared, or is parliamentary sovereignty with all its history sacrosanct and supreme? It involved issues of migration and border control, in what is one of the most crowded countries in the world. It involved issues about commercial trade offs: how important to British exports was membership of the Single Market, and how easily could Britain negotiate a suite of trade agreements with the rest of the world? And there were issues of geopolitics: is NATO sufficient for Britain's geopolitical security, or was membership of the EU necessary to ensure that the British voice continued to have influence?

Finally, though almost completely undiscussed, it involved issues of identity: who are we? Are we Europeans, and is that inevitably the same as being citizens of the EU? Or are we at some level so different that we can and should strike out on our own course in the world?

The months following the referendum and before Article 50 was triggered were a period of frantic preparation. The game plan needed to be readied, amid a din of public comment and special pleading. There were Brexit voters who, like the elephant, knew one big thing: they wanted to get out of the EU, and as quickly as possible. So anything that seemed to interfere with that was anathema: thus, for example, High Court judges who ruled that parliament was indeed sovereign in this matter were incredibly – according to the hysteria of the Brexit media – 'enemies of the people'. Then there were the foxes, who knew lots of little – or rather, more specific – things: the importance of the Single Market; the need to preserve London's role as the financial capital of Europe; the vital importance of Britain's world-class universities and their need to attract the best and the brightest from anywhere; the moral imperative to look after those EU citizens who had made their lives in Britain (and those Britons who had made theirs elsewhere in the EU); and the overwhelming desire to avoid the border on Ireland becoming real again, with all its threatening implications for the vulnerable peace that had been planted by the Good Friday Agreement.

All these voices, and more, filled the echo chamber in which government sought to make policy for a new world no one had planned for because no one had expected it. It all laid bare the enormous complexity of the task that lay ahead. But gradually over the months, government strategy coalesced around a vision of a new Global Britain that would be more open, more agile, more focussed on broader horizons and untrammelled by the sclerotic structures of the EU.

This new strategy is in effect an answer to the question about identity. It proposes nothing less than the most fundamental reorientation of Britain since the Second World War. It aims at a new identity.

Or is it an older one? And is that identity mature and robust enough to survive and prosper in the twenty-first century? There has been no shortage of discussion about what the eventual outcome of the negotiations with the EU will or should look like. The aim of this essay is not to offer more such speculation. Rather, it is to confront two critical questions about the British identity which have been exposed by the referendum, its aftermath and the new course the country is now seeking to chart at this moment when history is, for better or worse, unfrozen. One has received plenty of attention; the other has received very little, and yet is of even more fundamental importance. Both questions bear on the viability of Global Britain in the coming decades.

Individuals have identities which have an inner and an outward dimension. We all know from our experience of ourselves and of others that identities can be more or less mature, depending on whether they are more or less at ease with themselves and with others. 'Who do I think I am?' is thus two questions – about our inner and our outward person. The first question is the one we ask of the face in the mirror; the second is the one whose answer we read in the faces of others. And what is true for individuals holds in some way for societies and for nations: 'Who do we think we are?' Identity has both an inner and an outward dimension, for societies and for nations as well as for individuals.

So we can meaningfully ask two questions of the newly emerging post-EU Britain. First, about its inner dimension: what is the state of British society in the early years of the twenty-first century; what sort of people have we become? Second, about the external dimension of the British identity: what is the persona we present to others? These questions are related, and we need an honest confrontation with what the Brexit vote tells us about both if Britain is to succeed in charting a successful new course in the world, whatever the actual results of its negotiations with the EU and with other countries in the coming years.

The British in the mirror: what have we become?

What does the vote tell us about the sort of society we are? To see why it matters that we ask this question after Brexit, we only have to ask another question: why, in fact, was it such a shock? For a Remainer like myself it was certainly a disappointment. And I admit that it was a surprise. But why was it not just a surprise but a profound shock? After all, the opinion polls had clearly shown that the race was neck and neck. The result was within the margin of error of virtually every poll over at least the previous fortnight or so. Yet it was shocking: over the weekend after the result, even some of the prominent leaders of the Leave campaign appeared shocked by what had happened. Why?

It was a shock because we hadn't understood how divided the country was. Provincial against metropolitan; new economy against old; Scotland, London and Northern Ireland (of which more later) against much of the rest of England and Wales. The overall result was close; but few of the results by area were close – most were decisively, even strongly, one way or the other. Two London boroughs – Lambeth and Hackney – produced the largest Remain majorities in the country, at over 70%. (And they were by no means the most prosperous London boroughs; their voice was not the voice of the elite.) Every single area of Scotland voted to remain. The East and the East Midlands, on the other hand, produced the areas with the largest Leave votes in the country – also over 70%. The impact of urbanisation was mixed: smaller towns mostly voted to leave; the big cities mostly voted to remain (though Birmingham, by a narrow majority, did not). And there was a bizarrely inverse correlation between the amount of EU support funding received and the propensity to vote to remain.

This was also a vote of the old against the young. The correlation with age was very strong, with the old voting overwhelmingly to leave and the young overwhelmingly to remain; had the young been as enthusiastic to vote as the old – and particularly if the sixteen-year-olds had been given the vote, as they had been in Scotland two years before – they might have swung the result in the other direction. This fact is part of the explanation for the fury of the campaign and for the shock of the result: other things being equal, the demographic trends suggested that this was probably the last time the Brexit campaign could have won.

In other respects too, the picture was complex: income level and educational attainment were also strong indicators (though not gender). And the vote was to a surprising extent blind to party preference (moreover, many voted who had not bothered to vote in the general election the previous year). But above all, what this referendum really displayed was the extent of the distance between most of the British establishment – which includes Westminster and Whitehall, the City, big business, academia and the professional middle classes – and much of the rest of England and Wales (though not Scotland). And that has rung alarm bells, as indeed it should.

But it is important to recognise what is distinctive about this very British snapshot. In the months that followed, many argued that the Brexit vote was part of a worldwide phenomenon: the upset vote for Trump in the US in November 2016, the failure of the Italian constitutional referendum in December, and strong showings by anti-establishment groups in various European states before and since. These were all bracketed with the Brexit vote as evidence of a worldwide mood of alienation from globalisation and the liberal market consensus.

This is too simple, however. The Brexit vote, unlike the Trump vote, was not anti-trade: in that sense, it was not inward looking. To the contrary, the Brexit campaigners promised a more open Britain that would be the standard bearer for international trade policies that would energise the global economy, as well as revitalising Britain. Theirs was not a campaign against cheap Chinese imports. The contrast between the rhetoric of US politics and that of Britain in 2016 was unmistakable. Moreover, the animus of Brexit was quite different from that of the Italian rebellion: Britons were not voting to stop the radical overhaul of an inefficient state with enormous decentralised patronage powers, but more simply to keep Brussels out of their affairs and to control their borders. It was a vote against strangers being able to wander freely in their midst, not against trade and not against the country's own governance.

None of this makes it any less of a shock. Indeed, one deeply shaming reason for the shock was the upsurge in racial abuse, violence and even murder that preceded and followed the result. People who had lived in Britain for years experienced wholly gratuitous abuse or were made to feel uncomfortable and unwelcome. It was as if too many people felt they had suddenly been given permission to abuse the stranger among them.

We learn by reflecting on the past, and by recognising individual and collective failures. There is plenty of scope for debate about what exactly those failures are, but they certainly include all the sins of omission and commission which have resulted in a society deeply unequal in life chances, and in which many feel resentful and alienated. Britain is a very unequal society, on almost any measure. The degree of income inequality widened significantly in the last few decades of the twentieth century (albeit not in the last ten years), and is wider than that of all its major European peers (though less than that of the US). This inequality manifests itself in lower social mobility than in most of our major Western European peers.* More than in France or Germany, for example, the parents' position in the national income distribution determines the child's place in that distribution a generation later. This means that life chances are more skewed too. More than in either France or Germany, most of the rich have traditionally bought their way out of what they perceive as a mediocre state education system, in order to give their children a better start.

---

* The UK conforms neatly to the pattern known as the 'Great Gatsby' effect: income inequality is a strong inverse predictor of social mobility. (Strikingly, the US does too: the vaunted land of opportunity is even more unequal, but hardly any more socially mobile, than the UK.)

Much has undoubtedly changed for the better in British society over recent decades. If we suddenly found ourselves transported back half a century to the 1960s, we would be astonished and appalled by the class ridden, sexist and racist culture we would confront. Television satire of the time was beginning to expose and challenge this culture – see, for example, the series of 'I Know My Place' sketches in which Cleese, Barker and Corbett send up the nexus between accent, education, job, and attitude to life in general which bedevilled that era. (Even the differences in height of the three men told the story.) And we would now wince at the sharp-edged satire of 'Till Death Us Do Part', which cut so near the bone that not everyone recognised it for what it was, and which regularly provoked howls of both outrage and hilarity. We have travelled a long way from the world and the time they so mercilessly ridiculed.

Moreover, Britain fares well in many comparisons with its European peers. Overall, Britain is a mediocre performer by Western European standards in the key indices of health, education and social wellbeing. But the best British universities regularly appear in the top ten of the world: no continental university does so. Britain also has some of Europe and the world's leading specialist hospitals and medical research centres. And there are plenty of engaging characteristics of British society that stand comparison with others: Britons, for example, are more generous with voluntary contributions to charity than any of our European friends (though well behind the US). No country has a richer cultural offering: the BBC, for instance, broadcasts more live classical music than anywhere else in the world. And in London Britain has measurably the most cosmopolitan city in Europe – and indeed, arguably, on the planet.

But there is an underlying malaise, all the same. Britain has lived for half a century not only with an increasingly unequal society but also with an increasingly unbalanced economy. These two trends are related: for we have failed over decades to invest properly in the country's societal future, above all through the education and training needed to enhance life chances and social mobility.

Changes in the nature and structure of the economy in the latter decades of the last century have played their part in this, and the radical change in technology which is likely to transform the economy over the next few decades will exacerbate the challenge. The last generation has seen the British economy become more dominated by services than any other major European country: others have seen manufacturing decline as a percentage of national output in the face of newly globalised competition, but none as steeply as Britain. And as the share of manufacturing shrank from the 1970s onwards, apprenticeship training, which was the principal route into the good intermediate skilled jobs that are the backbone of any effective manufacturing industry, was allowed to wither on the vine.

Furthermore the service sectors, for all that they have prospered relative to manufacturing, are now increasingly subject to the winds of technological change too. Large numbers of intermediate skilled jobs have disappeared from the service sector, as well as from manufacturing, under the relentless impact of digitisation. The result is increasingly a two-tier labour market: those with a good start in life have the benefit of an economic growth path which provides highly lucrative jobs for barristers (and other roles which require high skills and major human investment) and a much larger number of poorly paid jobs for baristas (and many other low productivity roles that require little human investment).

Not that this 'hour glass' economy has done away with the need for intermediate skills. And in fact it is gradually building up a significant skills mismatch. An unbalanced and unfair system of preparation for adult working life has produced plenty of low-skilled workers but not enough intermediate skilled ones: over the next few years, Britain is likely to suffer from an excess supply of the former and a damaging shortage of the latter.* In an underinvested economy which has seen no material growth of labour productivity, economic growth overall has failed to increase average prosperity, and has been possible at all only because skills gaps have been plugged through immigration. Unemployment has been significantly lower than in virtually all of Britain's European peers and economic growth has therefore been effectively a function of demographic growth – in which immigration has played a prominent part. A large majority of all new jobs during the years since the financial and economic crisis have been filled through immigration, which has provided the skills that Britain needed in a whole range of sectors from health to construction.

At the same time, Britain's economy has built up one of the largest trade deficits in the world. Its goods exports have

---

* See the Social Mobility Commission: 'State of the Nation 2016', page xi.

lagged badly behind its major European peers, and although many service sectors – and above all, financial and professional services – have been highly successful in international markets, this has rarely been enough to offset the country's insatiable thirst for goods imports. So Britain has lived beyond its means for years, running a yawning trade deficit that has been covered partly by net dividends on its international investments and partly by capital inflows, which always come at a price.

This is not sustainable, and the social implications of these imbalances are certainly unacceptable. This is a complex problem with deep roots, both societal and economic. The Social Mobility Commission's report on 'The State of the Nation 2016' documents in sobering detail how a disadvantaged start in life feeds through into weaker average educational performance from the earliest years onwards; into less access to tertiary education (whilst at the same time there is less support for vocational development routes into adult working life); and hence into a labour market where the supply-demand equation is increasingly weighted against the low skilled.

This cycle might not seem so hard to break if Britain's educational system were outstanding. The peaks of British education are indeed magnificent, not only at the tertiary level but also in some of the academic hothouses of independent secondary education. But the fact is that on the most sophisticated measures of relative international educational performance in science, reading and mathematics, Britain is a middle-of-the-pack performer. British teenagers rank only 15th in science, 21st in reading and 27th in mathematics, amongst the 72 countries which take part in a triennial survey carried out by the OECD.* This is not the basis for an effective assault on the social immobility that has disfigured British society for so long.

What is more, the problem may be getting worse. For the young now face a housing market which is dramatically divided between the haves and the have-nots, as never before. The huge shortage of housing is now a fundamental obstacle to mobility and therefore a major contributor to enduring inequality. The imbalance is manifested in the sharp fall in home ownership amongst the young in recent years. The result is a new, and intractable, social divide marked by age, for older generations got on the first rung of the ladder when it was still affordable; by geography, as the divergence between the South East and the rest of the country has widened into a chasm; and by parental wealth, which many young people rely on to get into the housing market. Social mobility in the UK may now actually be getting worse.

All this is part of the background to the issue that came to dominate the Brexit campaign. Britain has been a natural magnet for immigration. On the whole it has been hospitable to newcomers. It has demonstrated a far-from-perfect, but nonetheless relatively easy-going, openness to the world at large. It has offered stable living in a prosperous society to

---

* The UK is ahead of the OECD average in science, and very slightly ahead in reading and mathematics. It is ahead of France in science and about the same in reading and mathematics; it trails Germany, and most of the other major European economies except Italy, in reading and mathematics.

immigrants from sometimes turbulent backgrounds in parts of the Commonwealth, to immigrants from a newly liberated but poor Eastern Europe, to professionals from Western Europe, and indeed from all corners of the world. In particular, the young and students have flocked to Britain in vast numbers, lured by the prize, not just of easy jobs, but of the English language.

We should not have been surprised that this became the fundamental concern of the Brexit campaign. It was nurtured against a background of perceived economic unfairness and exclusion, perhaps particularly in old economy areas where society had never really recovered from the rapid deindustrialisation of the 1980s. In 2015, the net number of immigrants was 333,000 – a figure that was published just weeks before the referendum. The figure has averaged over 200,000 a year for the last ten years, which amounts to a new city the size of Birmingham every five years. There has never been a mature national conversation about the kinds of challenges this might pose to the social and even the physical fabric of the country. The divisive problem of housing is just one of its manifestations. A concerted, broad-based and long-term policy response in the areas of housing, skills development and infrastructure investment could have met those challenges. But whatever progress has been made over the last two decades has not been sufficient to lay to rest the fears and the resentments. The consequence was a rebellion against an establishment that was perceived to have handed the keys to Brussels. One way of putting it was that we had lost sovereignty; the other was that there were too many strangers in our midst.

Brexit and Global Britain?

Britain's identity crisis has an external as well as an internal dimension. What was all this doing to our understanding of our place in the world? When we looked inward, in the mirror, we were shocked at what we saw, and learned something about what we have become. But were we any more ready to face our outward persona – to see our identity in the faces of others?

Brexit revealed something about the British that the establishment had tried to downplay for decades. For it was not simply the inevitable reaction of voters fed on a regular diet of bile about a meddlesome Commission, posturing by the European Parliament, ponderous rulings from the European Court of Justice, pork barrel politicking by the member states, the self-inflicted travails of the Eurozone, and much else that seemed to demonstrate the unaccountable distance and incompetence of the EU. The vote reflected all this, certainly, but more than that, it was a vote about our identity.

The Brexit rebellion did not come out of the blue. In fact, it was more than sixty years in the making. This is not the place to discuss the viability of the EU and its ability to confront the many challenges Europeans face in a world in which the centre of gravity has moved away from Europe, never to return. The truth is, of course, that it is gravely underprepared, and even its most ardent advocates in the Remain camp knew that it needs radical reform.* How different the EU, which so many of us love to hate, could have been. How much better it could have been, if only Britain had engaged wholeheartedly from the start and led the shaping of it at a time when Britain's influence would have been dominant in Western Europe, and when the United States clearly wanted to see a new cohesiveness which would allow Europe to prosper as a bulwark against the Soviet Empire to the east. How much better for Europe; how much better the options could have been for the people of this country too.

But for forty years, British political leaders have treated Brussels as a convenient whipping boy for all sorts of actual or perceived ills inflicted on their citizenry. And for more than sixty years, the British political class (of both the left and the right) has shown a shortsightedness and indeed dishonesty about Britain's strategic options in Europe and in the wider world, ever since the years when the founders of the European project sought to create a new and peaceful postwar order. Our forebears were still at that time fixated by empire and its aftermath. Famously, Churchill told parliament in 1943 that he had not become His Majesty's First Minister in order to preside over the dissolution of the British Empire. For him, Britain still had a global role to play after the catastrophe. His remarkably farsighted speech of September 1946, delivered at

---

* The response in the EU and in its member states to the British withdrawal has been a mixture of regret and anger. Official reaction has circled the wagons: there has been relatively little appetite for deep and honest reflection about the implications for the European project of the fact that the second biggest member state has chosen to leave.

the University of Zurich, argued for the creation of a United States of Europe. Strikingly, given that this was little more than a year after the end of the war, whilst Germany was still prostrate in total physical and moral collapse, he called for this new European project to be jointly led by its two natural leaders – and ancient enemies – France and Germany. But not for a moment did he consider that Britain should join in. A blessing from the sidelines was what he offered, nothing more.

For Britain saw itself as scanning different horizons, even as it came to terms with the loss of India. It was still the heart of an empire, the mother country of the Commonwealth, and the cousin and special relation of the United States. It was also the would-be champion of a more open, global trading order; and to this end it believed that its key international economic objective was the reestablishment of sterling as a global reserve currency. Technically, this translated into a medium-term objective of convertibility; and this meant that financial objectives dominated its international economic priorities. Intrinsic to this mindset was a tendency to underestimate the potential of European commercial relationships, not least because Britain saw itself as the hub of an international network, the legacy of empire, which could meet its needs for food and raw materials and for export markets.

This was not just the voice of mercantilism or of the arch imperialist Churchill. This was a deeply embedded self-understanding, widely shared in British public opinion across all classes and backgrounds, and carrying clear implications for Britain's postwar international strategy. The new Labour government in 1945 bought into it with little reservation. In particular, Ernie Bevin – that bull elephant of a man who was Foreign Secretary for almost all the government's life – turned out to be almost a spiritual cousin of the Etonian Anthony Eden whom he replaced. His attitude to Jean Monnet and the architects of the new European project was condescending and dismissive. The project was for those who had been beaten by war, not for the undefeated, and it would probably not succeed anyway. Britain's future lay in its independent role on the world stage, flagged by its renewed presence east of Suez and by its permanent seat and veto on the Security Council of the new United Nations.

The deep flaws in this view of Britain's place in the world are obvious, at least in hindsight. It exaggerated the importance of Britain to the US and it assumed that loyalty and affection within the Commonwealth would translate into shared interests. It led Britain's political elite to overlook the significance of what was happening in Europe: as a result, its overall aims and tactics were badly misjudged. During the 1950s, Britain's policy towards the emerging European project went through three phases which, taken as a whole, can only be described as a comprehensive strategic failure*:

---

* With the critical exception of security policy, where the British clearly recognised the importance of NATO as a structure which would keep the Americans committed in Europe. NATO's success in its primary objectives is too easily taken for granted: the failed European Defence Community would surely have been a more risky venture. Few in Britain shed a tear for it when the French voted it down. But too many took this as evidence that no European project could succeed: in fact, however, the failure led to a renewed spurt of energy directed towards commercial collaboration, and the European

first, a benevolent neutrality underpinned by the unspoken hope that it would evaporate (particularly as France recovered its self-confidence on the world stage); then a phase of more determined efforts to undermine it, culminating in an official statement in 1955 that Britain would not join the nascent Common Market; and finally, a change of tack, when it became clear that the six founding members of the Common Market were indeed making progress towards a new West European economic structure. West German economic success was beginning to unnerve British industry; at the same time, the major Commonwealth countries were becoming less and less ready to assume that all roads led to London. All this led to a proposal for a European Free Trade Area that would include the Common Market of the Six within it.

This belated push for a new, more open trade framework orchestrated by London, which would embrace a Brussels-led Common Market, was a concession to reality by a country which had not wanted supranational economic structures to emerge in Europe but which then had to make the best of what was actually happening. Not surprisingly, it evoked suspicion about Britain's real commitment to Europe, and it failed after months of negotiations in 1958. The Six went ahead and signed the Treaty of Rome without Britain; meanwhile, sterling's new convertibility simply helped to expose Britain's weakening financial and commercial position. Britain finally applied to join the club in 1961 only to run into Charles de

---

project advanced towards the Common Market despite the failure of the EDC.

Gaulle's infamous veto: France had indeed recovered its self-confidence, and was now in the political driving seat which could have been Britain's.

The comparison with France is instructive. France had had its moral authority and self-confidence shaken by the experience of the war much more brutally than Britain. It, too, found it difficult to reconcile itself to the loss of empire – and its loss was more deeply traumatic – in Vietnam but above all in Algeria. But despite all the pain, France was no more reconciled than Britain was to being just one of several European countries. It is part of the identity of both that they are different from others. De Gaulle's political testament began with a famous opening sentence: 'All my life I have always had a certain idea of France.'* Like Britain, France was determined to recover its global poise, to have its own seat at the top table in the United Nations and to retain the ability to project hard power. But France also knew that it had no choice about the European project. Unlike Britain, it could not delude itself that there were alternative paths. So it determined to lead the project. To France, it was a new basis for French authority on the world stage; for Britain the application to join felt more like a confession of failure on that stage.

As Gorbachov said to his East German hosts in October 1989, history punishes those who come too late. At that point, Britain had been a member of the EEC for less than two decades. In its first decade as a member, its influence was gravely weakened by its own dire economic condition. In its second decade, it became more assertive and influential in

---

* Charles de Gaulle, *Mémoires de Guerre*, 1954.

driving the creation of the Single Market. But then there followed two historic European reunifications: first of Germany and then of Europe as a whole, as the countries of Eastern and Central Europe came back into the mainstream of European political, cultural and economic life. This brought Germany to the centre of the European stage, both geographically and politically. Now the leadership of the European project was no longer in the hands of the French (who had no more wanted to submerge their identity in a wider European sea than did the British); it was now ever more obviously in the hands of a much more deeply integrationist Germany. And with the birth of the Eurozone, the European project took on a new complexity and momentum. All this was increasingly troubling for a Britain which not only had genuine (and well-founded) concerns about the wisdom of introducing a common currency, but which had also – more fundamentally – never really stopped looking over its shoulder even as it turned its hand to the plough.

After Edward Heath, Britain had only one Prime Minister with a European vision which went beyond economics and who was at ease with the European project: Tony Blair. There was a moment when he might even have taken Britain into the Eurozone, not purely on economic grounds but to keep Britain at the centre of European affairs. Had other circumstances been different, he might have played the role of the elder statesman and passionate advocate for the Remain campaign, rather as Gordon Brown did for the Union in the Scottish independence referendum. That was not to be.

The fact is that since the war, from Churchill and Attlee onwards, the gut instinct and the rhetoric of almost all the

British political class has been to treat the European project as, at best, a commercial opportunity (or necessity), not as Britain's destiny. In this they were in tune with a British self-awareness that was measurably less inclined to see itself as European than any of its neighbours. That self-awareness, that identity, has evolved over the years, to be sure. But tragically, it was most conspicuously out of line with reality during the all-important postwar period. And the British political class, which should have been prepared to acknowledge the home truths, to help the country confront them, to set out a new vision which was both compelling and realistic, and to chart the country's course accordingly, failed to do so – especially during the crucial ten years that led up to the signature of the Treaty of Rome in 1958. We live with the consequences still: we took ourselves off the bridge over half a century ago, and Britain's ability to influence the European project has been limited ever since. Europe is the worse for it, and so are we. The Brexit vote and the proposed new identity of 'Global Britain' is the latest chapter in Britain's search for a role in which it can find a secure identity. And no one other than a few ideologues can be confident that the search has reached its end.

The history that weighs on Britain

At the deepest level of human consciousness, identity is always moulded by the Other. At a societal level, defining the Other means – however inchoately – being able to define who is part of the community and who is not. At the national level, it means, not just controlling who can come in, but – again, however inchoately – identifying the international Other. A secure identity, whether for individual human beings or for communities or for nations, is a secure relationship with the Other. And this has to rest on three pillars: realism about context, about history, and about familial and/or cultural affinities.

Britain's identity today is fragile because all three of its pillars are fragile. It would take too much space in this short essay to argue this point in full detail.* But, as we have just seen, the British political class showed all too little realism about context when it mattered crucially in the years after the Second World War. Moreover, the history – including the

---

* Identity has been the subject of lively philosophical debate from classical Greek and Roman times onwards, as a question with metaphysical, psychological, sociological and ethical dimensions. And from Augustine onwards, through Locke and into modern times, the importance of memory and history, both personal and collective, in forming and defining identity has been ever more clearly understood.

deep history – that coloured British dreams then continues to weigh heavily on the present. We will come later to note how this in turn shapes British perceptions about the affinities that bind it together, and about what determines the difference between friends and strangers. But before doing so, we need to look more closely at the role of history in the British identity.

Questions about identity are always – and most surely in Britain's case – caught up in a tangle of history. Not always fully understood or acknowledged, and therefore all the more subtly influential, history weighed heavily on the Brexit vote. Churchillian turns of phrase and references to the great traditions going back all the way to the Magna Carta (whose eight hundredth anniversary had been celebrated the previous year) filled the air. The shadows cast by history were everywhere. And it is clear that this was not new; this same history had weighed on the political class in the years after the war too.

Hence, there are questions that we must ask ourselves about that history. For if we were to focus just on the policies and practices of the British establishment over the last few decades, important though they undoubtedly were, then we would miss some of the most uncomfortable truths about ourselves. For we British have not been living wholly honestly with our past. It is crucial to recognise that this is not a case where one side in the debate was a prisoner of the past and the other free of it. Most of the Churchillian rhetoric came from the Leavers, who were certainly resonating with deeply rooted public attitudes and the pervasive sense of 'otherness' from Europe. But the fact that the Remainers argued almost entirely on the basis of economic calculus, and often as though the EU were Britain's least worst option, shows in effect that they subscribed to the same basic view of Britain's identity. Whether we feel we are members of the establishment or whether we feel alienated from it and mistrustful of it – in either case, too many of us have lived for too long with a general sense that we can be proud of our history and of the distinctive role Britain has played in European and in global history.

And indeed, there is much to be proud of: yes, we did stand alone against the evil of the Third Reich in May 1940. Yes, we did bring a halt to Napoleon's vaulting ambition at Waterloo (albeit with the crucial help of the Prussians). Yes, it was Britons who led the campaign for abolition of the slave trade, and it was the Royal Navy that enforced it on the high seas. Yes, we have had a continuously adjusting constitution ever since the signing of the Magna Carta, which has given us the mother of parliaments and enough flexibility – at least since the English Civil War – to avoid the brittleness of French, German, Italian or Spanish political history. Yes, our common law, evolving over centuries and upheld by an independent judiciary is – in the words of W.S.Gilbert – the true embodiment of everything that's excellent.* Yes, we are the

---

* 'The Law is the true embodiment/ Of everything that's excellent./ It has no kind of fault or flaw/ And I, my Lords, embody the Law', so sings the Lord Chancellor, in Iolanthe. The gentle satire of British establishment life which keeps audiences of Gilbert and Sullivan delighted to this day is itself a manifestation of one of Britain's most engaging characteristics.

heirs of Shakespeare and our language has become the lingua franca of the planet. And yes, we are the heirs of a culture which values pragmatism more than doctrine, manifest, for example, in the Elizabethan Anglican settlement that became a veritable study in what both its admirers and detractors call compromise.*

But the fact is that there are other things on the scales too. For this was also the country whose foreign policy from the nineteenth century onwards was conducted with what can only, from our present vantage point, be described as breathtaking arrogance. For a brief half-century or so, from Waterloo in 1815 to the unification of Germany in 1871, Britain was the most powerful nation on the planet. And no one represented that power more forcefully and eloquently than Lord Palmerston, variously Foreign Secretary and Prime Minister for twenty-four of those years. His high-handedness made him enemies in the British establishment, but he knew how to play to the gallery, as evidenced by the famous speech in parliament in 1848 that laid out his philosophy:

> It is a narrow policy to suppose that this country or that is to be marked out as the eternal ally or the perpetual

---

* The deliberate fudge on a key doctrinal point that was tearing European Christendom apart at the time – the nature and meaning of the Eucharist – is the locus classicus. This does not, of course, mean that all was sweetness and light: Anglican treatment of Catholics and of Protestant Dissenters until well into the nineteenth century left plenty to be desired.

enemy of England.* We have no eternal allies, and we have no perpetual enemies. Our interests are eternal and perpetual, and those interests it is our duty to follow.

This comes after a passage where Palmerston argues that:

England is a power sufficiently strong to steer her own course, and not to tie herself as an unnecessary appendage to the policy of any other government. I hold that the real policy of England – apart from questions which involve her own particular interests, political or commercial – is to be the champion of justice and right; pursuing that course with moderation and prudence, not becoming the Quixote of the world, but giving the weight of her moral sanction and support wherever she thinks that justice is, and wherever she thinks that wrong has been done.

This passage is telling: it reveals the capacity for double-think that was so typical of the British in empire.† To be the champion of justice and right: that was Britain's role as the

---

* Palmerston, who held an Irish peerage, was, like most other establishment figures then and down the years since until very recently, untroubled by the use of the name 'England' for the kingdom.

† This is not to argue that the British have been the only ones capable of doublethink: the passage could just as well describe the approach of the United States in the postwar period – or even that of the Chinese government now, as they argue vociferously for the contribution their 'one belt, one road' policy will make to regional peace and prosperity (as well as to underpinning Chinese influence in the region).

world's superpower – but with the all-important exception of where her own particular interests are involved, whether political or commercial (and those were rarely far apart). This was not simply specious: Palmerston was a lifelong abolitionist, determined that the Royal Navy should police the seas and stop any vessel from any country, whether allied, neutral or hostile, suspected of carrying slaves. But it was a long way from unsullied virtue either: those particular interests for which Palmerston made exception had been in play just a few years earlier, for example, during the First Opium War.

As for the core philosophy – no eternal allies, only eternal and perpetual interests – not only was this wrong even in its own terms (Palmerston clearly defined the British presence in India as a permanent interest), but more generally, it reduces all international relationships to pure contracts. How much wiser (and, indeed, ironically appropriate in this context) were the famous words of John Donne over two centuries earlier: no man is an island entire of itself, but every man a piece of the continent.* He meant this in the context of individual human relationships: that we are not just autonomous individuals, but that we are connected deeply, that we are 'involved in mankind'. But as individuals we are members of communities, of societies, and – as matters stand, at least – citizens of nations. What he said applies not only to individuals but also to the communities, the societies, the nations we are part of. Identities do not exist, and cannot flourish, in isolation.

---

* From his 'Meditation XVII', *Devotions upon Emergent Occasions*, 1624.

There is a still more basic question to be asked: where does the notion of Britain itself come from? For though the country is old, its identity as Britain is not. Britannia was the old Roman name for the island, of course, and the pre-Roman inhabitants were known as Britons. But the Britons were marginalised by waves of newcomers – Angles and Saxons, Gaelic Scots, and the Norse. It was the Anglo-Saxon settlers who gave their name to England, and the Scottish Gaels who gave their name to Scotland. The ancient Britons had their heirs in the Welsh, the Cornish and the Manx. But as the kingdoms of England and Scotland coalesced over the Middle Ages, no one called themselves British. All the way through to Tudor England and Stuart Scotland, they remained two proudly separate kingdoms. Their struggles with each other and their jockeying in their relationships with others, especially France and Spain, are the stuff of folklore. It is not until the union of the two crowns in the one person of James the Sixth of Scotland and First of England that Great Britain starts to take on a real identity. James wanted to be the king of Great Britain and proclaimed himself as such, even though he could not get parliamentary endorsement for the title. The seeds of a new identity had been sown; but the seventeenth century was a time of religious and constitutional turmoil that absorbed all the energy of England, whilst religious and political infighting bedevilled the elite of Edinburgh. So it was almost another century after James before the seeds of the new British identity began to sprout.

The ground was prepared by the catastrophic failure of a Scottish enterprise in the New World, which had consumed a significant proportion of the economic surplus of Scotland in a vain attempt to establish a trading colony in what is now Panama. The Scottish establishment had sought to do what the English, the French and the Dutch were doing as they fanned out over the oceans. The failure pushed them into the financial arms of London, and there followed the Act of Union. The closure of the Scottish Parliament in 1707 was bitterly opposed by some*: but a new, albeit fragile, identity had been established. Subsequent rebellions in Scotland were aimed at reinstalling the House of Stuart, not at reestablishing an independent Scotland – even if they generated a new chapter of Scottish folklore centred on Bonny Prince Charlie. And in fact, Scottish intellectual life flourished in the new Union, even as the language and symbols of the ancient highland Scottish traditions were being suppressed after Culloden. Scots played leading roles in forming the new Great British identity, not least by heading overseas in their thousands under the aegis of the East India Company, as the British government deliberately used its powers of patronage in the Company to provide outlets for Scottish energy and thus to quell any risk of discontent which might threaten the Union.

And what of the other great island of the British Isles? The Romans never reached Hibernia. But Latin Christianity did, creating a monastic culture which flourished and exported its learning and its distinctive expression of Christian worship

---

* In 1713, one year before the arrival on the new British throne of James' great-grandson, George I, as the first Hannoverian king, an attempt to overturn the Union failed in the House of Lords by just four votes.

into Scotland and the north of England. Like England and Scotland, Ireland suffered from destructive Viking raiding, which there – as elsewhere – led in some cases to settlements permanent enough to be known by Viking names (not least Dublin). Then came the Normans from their English bastions; this ushered in a chaotic period of struggle amongst Norman lords and Irish chieftains, whilst successive kings of England were determined that no one should succeed in setting up a competing state in Ireland. Direct rule began with the first Tudor, Henry VII, under a statute known as Poynings' Law.* Henry VIII took the final step, proclaiming himself King of Ireland in 1541, as a prelude to a sustained English effort to establish effective control over the whole island – something no one, either Irish or Norman, had succeeded in doing before.

From that point onwards, Ireland was set on the course that was to turn it into Britain's most shameful and traumatic colonial experience. It took a century and a half of brutality in the face of repeated resistance and rebellion to establish control. By the eighteenth century, the most that could be said was that the savagery was over. The Catholic Irish peasantry – whom the Anglican landowning elite had no success

---

* After Sir Edward Poynings, the appointed deputy of Henry VII in his capacity as Lord of Ireland. The law provided that the Irish Parliament could not legislate without the prior approval of the English monarch in Privy Council. This law was to bedevil relations between the Westminster and Dublin parliaments all the way through to the end of the eighteenth century when the Irish Parliament was finally abolished.

in converting – were patronised, exploited and deathly poor. Plague and famine repeatedly ravaged them. Meanwhile, the deliberate settlement of Scottish and English Protestant Presbyterians on expropriated land in the north sowed seeds of cultural bigotry from which later generations have reaped a whirlwind.

Not that Ireland played no part in the blossoming life of the new Britain of the eighteenth century. George Berkeley, the Anglican bishop and empiricist philosopher; Jonathan Swift, the master satirist and pamphleteer; Edmund Burke, the great statesman and philosophical opponent of the French revolution – these were all Irishmen who had a profound influence on the British identity. And Georgian Dublin became an intellectual centre (and architectural treasure), which bore respectful comparison with Edinburgh. By the time of George IV, motifs linking the shamrock with the rose and the thistle were to be seen in London architecture and on royal jewellery.*

Yet despite all this, Ireland was at no point successfully embraced by the new British identity. Scotland did well out of union; Ireland did not. Economically as well as culturally, Scotland was enriched; Ireland was impoverished. Two false dawns ended badly: the first came in the 1780s when the charismatic Irish leader Henry Grattan, supported by Pitt, won back a measure of authority for the Irish Parliament, only for the French Revolution to inspire uprisings which

---

* See, for example, the Water Gate at Greenwich Palace, or the royal diadem worn first by George IV and still shown being worn by Elizabeth II on British postage stamps.

then led instead to its closure. The second came in the 1880s, when another charismatic Irishman, Charles Stuart Parnell, working with Gladstone, might have argued the British Parliament into conceding home rule – before he was brought down by his famous affair with Kitty O'Shea.*

Notwithstanding the travails of Ireland, however, the blossoming of the new Great Britain was the beginning of a vibrant period – a time of industrial inventiveness, scientific progress, Enlightenment philosophy, missionary zeal and trade. These were the times when the British identity took shape and began to assert itself. The British Museum was founded in 1753; the *Encyclopaedia Britannica* was first published in Edinburgh in 1768. George III announced his patriotism as the new king in 1760 by declaring that he gloried in the name of Briton. Both London and Edinburgh were imprinted with the new image. William Chambers, the brilliant Scottish architect, built Somerset House to house the navy offices in premises – intended to be 'at once an object of national splendour as well as convenience'† – which were adorned by sculptures celebrating the oceanic ambitions, the genius and the energy of Great Britain. In Edinburgh, the New Town put the British royal family on the street plan

---

* Just opposite the headquarters building of the European Commission in Brussels stands a pub called the Kitty O'Shea. Very few of those who pass by every day on EU business will have any inkling of the connection of that name with this nineteenth-century British and Irish tragedy.

† From the Somerset House Guidebook, published by the Somerset House Trust, 2000.

(George Street, Charlotte Square, Princes Street), as well as giving the city some of its most spectacular architecture.

British energy brought success in trade around the world. The rejection of monarchical absolutism (at a time when this was just a dream in France or in the German lands) was accompanied by the rise of 'people of the middling sort' for whom trade and industry were the purpose of life. Over the next century they urbanised Britain and crossed the seas in pursuit of new markets. In some places they settled; in others they founded trading stations; and where they found local rulers who were weak, unreliable or unwelcoming, they were drawn in to occupation. The trajectory from the East India Company to full-scale British rule in India is the archetypal and central case. Trade supported by a navy which could reach anywhere in the world led to empire. Commercial ambition became inextricably entwined with national pride. 'Rule, Britannia!' by the Scottish poet and playwright James Thomson and set to its famous music by Thomas Arne, was first publicly performed in London in 1745. Its instant and enduring success sums up, more than any other cultural creation before the twentieth century, the new British identity: patriotic, outward looking and self-assertive.

But self-assertion is not the same as self-confidence. The passion for trade had mercantilist motives, born of a sense of vulnerability: Britain knew it could not be self-sufficient, and knew too that it was in fierce competition with others – especially the French – for markets. It was also insecure: the twin fears of absolute rule internally and of invasion from across the seas were always buried just below the surface of the elite's consciousness. Their libertarianism would never countenance the kind of standing army the Prussians, for example, gloried in. The navy, on the other hand, was a weapon of existential significance. Small wonder that it became the key symbol of Britain's identity. Britons would never be slaves, and Britannia was certainly going to rule the waves.

And so Britannia became the icon of a nineteenth-century imperialism whose most influential strategist was Lord Palmerston.* At its peak the British Empire spread further than any other empire since that of the Mongols. It has left a remarkable legacy: in much of its territory for much of the time, it provided stable and honest governance of those it ruled; it spread Britain's hard won legal system round the world; it educated elites on Enlightenment principles (which would eventually motivate many independence movements within the empire); and it played a major role in ensuring the preeminence of English, not only as the world's lingua franca but as the language which has borrowed (and been enriched by) more words from more languages than any other in the world.

At their best, the British in empire saw themselves as striving for the betterment of people's lives. Those who flocked from Britain to all the reaches of empire were not only traders, adventurers and chancers. They were not only

---

* The life experience of the newly urbanised poor in the nineteenth century was, of course, less of the large horizons opened up by trade and empire, and more of factories, the Poor Law and the workhouse. Nevertheless, Britain's position of empire became more and more important both to government policy and to the national self-awareness as the century wore on.

Clive, Rhodes and their like. They included highly intelligent and intellectually curious administrators like Warren Hastings and Stamford Raffles; they included brilliant orientalist scholars like Sir William Jones, and countless dedicated missionaries, educationalists, doctors, explorers, archaeologists and natural scientists.* But the nineteenth century also saw a growing arrogance based on Britain's own rising self-confidence, sense of racial superiority and belief in its national destiny. Not only would Britons never be slaves: they were born – they increasingly felt – to rule. This was the arrogance personified by Lord Lugard in Africa or by Lord Curzon in India. And at the same time they never lost that Palmerstonian consciousness of existential competition with the other European great powers, who also saw themselves as called to imperial destinies in Asia and Africa.

Overall, this British record in empire is a good deal more mixed than many of us are comfortable in recognising. Indians have a livelier folk memory of the Mutiny, of the partition of Bengal, of the Jallienwalla Bagh or of the 1943 Bengal famine – as well as of the indignity of a supercilious Raj in general – than the British care to believe. And the Chinese will regularly remind those of us who choose to forget about the opium wars, about the Unequal Treaties, about duplicity over Shandong at Versailles in 1919, and, again, about the indignity of being treated as social inferiors in Hong Kong,

---

* India is one of the best-documented natural environments anywhere in the world, as a result of a tradition of detailed field work begun by British naturalists as early as the seventeenth century.

Shanghai and elsewhere.* For the British today, all this seems a long time ago; for the Chinese, it was yesterday. Meanwhile in the Middle East, the history of British involvement from the beginning of the twentieth century onwards is filled with cynicism and duplicity, not to mention moments of sheer folly that still have the power to shock, not least because we are not familiar with the details. But the Iranians in particular certainly are, and remain wary to this day of the British (as well as of the Americans who were our partners in machinations over oil after the Second World War).

Recent years have seen a much greater readiness than before to stare these truths in the face. Penetrating critiques of imperialism were once mainly the preserve of Marxism. Now they are more often the work of historians who write with the benefit of perspective and without the baggage of Victorian and prewar prejudice; or of educated thinkers from what used to be the realms of empire, who speak up, often in nuanced terms and in the language of the Enlightenment and/or of cultural identity (Amartya Sen and Kwame Anthony Appiah are both prominent examples). But nevertheless, what remains – very broadly diffused through the modern British consciousness – is a warmish afterglow generated by a sense that Britain's record in the last two hundred years is on the whole a source of legitimate pride. This in turn nourishes a sense that Britain deserves a special place in the

---

* In Hong Kong the Chinese were banned from the famous Peak; in Shanghai, the notice at the gate of the Huangpu Park did not actually say 'no dogs or Chinese' but it did reserve the park for the foreign community and did ban dogs.

pantheon of the world – that we are not just a small country at the European end of the Eurasian landmass.

Unforeseen consequences

Britain's self-understanding as at the centre of a worldwide network of familial links outlived its role as the centre of empire. A hundred years before, at the zenith of British imperial power, Palmerston had articulated a doctrine of the British subject, in justification of a piece of swashbuckling gunboat diplomacy, by reference to a great and famous principle of the Roman Empire:

> As the Roman, in days of old, held himself free from indignity, when he could say, Civis Romanus sum, so also a British subject, in whatever land he may be, shall feel confident that the watchful eye and the strong arm of England will protect him from injustice and wrong.*

This had wider implications Palmerston never foresaw. If all the people of the British dominions were British subjects,

---

* The casus belli was the refusal of the Greek Government to compensate the Portuguese honorary consul in Athens for the vandalisation of his property by an anti-Semitic mob. The consul came from Gibraltar; Palmerston argued that he was thus entitled to the protection of the British Government, so he sent a naval squadron to force the Greek Government to pay up. (And notice, again, Palmerston's elision of Britain and England.)

this also meant that they could take up residence wherever they might want in those dominions. During the hundred years leading up to the Second World War, what that meant in practice was that large numbers of Britons left their homeland for a better life elsewhere. To this day, million of Britons have close relatives in Canada, Australia and New Zealand. But after the war, it also became the basis for flows in the opposite direction: in 1948, the passenger ship *Empire Windrush* brought the first 492 Caribbeans to seek a better life in Britain, on the basis of new legislation by the Attlee government which clarified their status and meant in effect that they could indeed see themselves as 'cives Britannici'.

People followed in large numbers from the Caribbean and from South Asia. And British culture has been profoundly changed as a result, so much so that it takes an effort of imagination to envisage the simpler, more monochrome Britain that existed before the war. The language, the cuisine, the social appearance of most British cities – all have been changed and enriched. There is, of course, nothing new about this. Down the ages, the island that is Britain had seen wave after wave of newcomers already: Romans, Saxons, Danes, Normans, Jews, Huguenots, Irish. Some came as invaders, some as refugees, some because they thought the streets were paved with gold. The British identity has been moulded by all of them.

The wave of immigration from the new Commonwealth in the postwar years was certainly not trouble free; Britain has had its share of prejudice, of race riots and – latterly – of religiously motivated terrorism. Within a generation of those first arrivals, British principles of citizenship were changed and made far more restrictive: it was the end of the imperial understanding of 'civis Britannicus'. But the old Britain had gone for good. There are still issues about integration, as well as debates about the values that define Britishness and about how (and indeed whether) they should be inculcated as a part of civic education. Nevertheless, what has become a highly diverse society from a standing start in less than seventy years now just seems normal. London is the largest case study: over two hundred languages are spoken on its streets every day; it is home to more people from more places than any other city in the world; over a third of its population was born outside the UK; and it now has a practicing Muslim as its mayor.

Why, then, was immigration the decisive issue in the Brexit vote? Was it just because the numbers involved in this latest wave – the wave of the twenty-first century – were large? Was it just because of the lack of control, given the freedom of movement enshrined in the EU constitution? Yes, these were factors; but they are equally surely not the whole truth. Nor can it be that Eastern Europeans posed a greater cultural and social assimilation challenge than those who came from the Commonwealth in the wake of the *Empire Windrush*. The clue to the deeper issue lies in the fact that there were so few voices even in the Remain camp who were prepared to argue their case in terms of a European identity. Why did the entire campaign, on both sides, implicitly presuppose that Britain is something other than – something more than – one of the leading member states of the EU? The answer is because that is what so many of the British feel.* The truth is

---

* The regular Eurobarometer surveys of public attitudes conducted by

that the British identity is still deeply imbued by its imperial past. And yes, perhaps that identity was at some level more at ease with a modern profile of Britain that had been so deeply impacted by the Commonwealth than with the new influx from Poland.*

---

the European Commission have always shown that UK citizens are less likely to think of themselves as European, either as a primary or even as a secondary identity, and more likely to think of themselves only in purely national terms, than in any other member state. This is true for every age cohort, for all levels of educational attainment, and in every socio-economic grouping. Tertiary level students and managers show the highest percentages of European identification, but still only at around 50% – and even in these categories, the proportion is well behind all other EU member states.

* Norman Tebbitt's famous cricketing test of national identity – who did people support when England was playing? – might have had a deeper resonance than he had in mind. The Caribbeans and the South Asians all play cricket: the Poles don't. (But it is hardly a Scottish passion either; so the test begs another question about the true nature of the British identity, which he presumably never intended.)

The ties that bind us

Yet this exposes an uncomfortable question about the subtle effect of this identity on Britain's understanding of its place in the world. Through all the imperial diversions and distractions of the two and a half centuries during which Britain has nurtured its identity, it has consistently had to be reminded that it is also European by virtue of geographical and cultural realities we cannot deny.

Zbigniew Brzezinski, the former American National Security Adviser, wrote a penetrating analysis of the geopolitics of Eurasia from the perspective of the US of the 1990s, at a time when it was indisputably the world's only global superpower.* He contrasts this American position with that of Britain in the nineteenth century, during the era when it had been heavily engaged in the great power games of Eurasia. The key difference, he argues, is that although Britain might rule the waves, it could never dominate Europe. What it sought there was a balance of continental powers, so that no one could threaten a Britain for whom Napoleon's continental system had been the stuff of nightmares for a generation. For a brief period from Waterloo until the unification of Prussian dominated Germany, Britain could safely pursue its aims elsewhere undistracted. But this was an interlude. The story

---

* Zbigniew Brzezinski, *The Grand Chessboard*, Basic Books, 1998.

of the last decades before the First World War is well enough known. The great lesson of 1914 is clear: Britain found that it could not avoid being involved in Europe, whatever its global pretensions. And the next generation had plenty of cause to remember this. The second war was truly global – but for Britain, though it might mean humiliation in the Far East, it was existential in Europe.

The question of European entanglement has by no means gone away. There is absolutely no reason to believe that any of the member states of the EU might revert to former behaviour patterns. Democracy is now deeply rooted, and the digital and travelling age has created a demos which will not be seduced by dreams of national glory of the kind to which our forbears succumbed in 1914. Yet the growing pains of the postwar European project are still very obvious. Though it is more likely to muddle through, it could break up in acrimony. If the earthquake happened, Britain would not escape the tidal wave. We can no more turn our back on the European project now than we could ignore the Continent in the last century.

But there is more: for the British identity has been fashioned by centuries of relationships with our European neighbours – relationships which are deeply rooted because they are about so much more than just trade and geopolitics. If we pretend that we can ignore this element of our identity, that we are just a member of the global community of nations, and that trading with the world is the be-all and end-all of a robust national identity, then we deceive ourselves about our own roots, and about who we really are. There is a profound threat to our identity in the way post-Brexit Britain proposes to present itself as 'Global Britain'.

These European relationships go back a long way. They call to mind a whole history of the European consciousness, in which the people of the British Isles have been closely involved. It is a consciousness whose roots lie in the early centuries of Latin Christianity. It has evolved through a readiness to broaden its intellectual horizons through its own restless metaphysical searching from Augustine onwards – by rediscovering the half-forgotten wisdom of classical Greece, by engaging with the brilliance of Islamic scholarship at its zenith in Muslim Spain, by its growing readiness to challenge redundant scientific orthodoxies, by rebutting any claims to divine right or to absolute authority on the part of any temporal power, and by gradually discovering the sanctity of the individual. As a result, Europe has common core values which have been hard won through history. They are the heritage of a tradition of thought which has been shaped by such towering figures as Aquinas, Luther, Erasmus, Galileo, Descartes, Locke, Hume, Rousseau, Kant, Hegel, Darwin – and of course many others too.

None of this came easily. The battles fought for truths we now hold to be self-evident were often bloody and drawn out. The sound and the fury of religious and post-Enlightenment ideological strife dominates much of European history. The outcome of centuries of conflict is that Europe is now at peace, even if afraid of an assertive and resurgent Asia, nervous about the cultural challenge posed by the growing presence of Islam in its midst, and – having lost touch with its Christian humanist origins and lost confidence in its Enlightenment heritage – unsure what it stands for in the modern world.

People from these islands have been heavily involved in all this from the earliest beginnings. Irish monks took Christian learning to the German lands; Anselm, Duns Scotus and William of Ockham were towering figures in the medieval European debate about metaphysics and the nature of things; Tyndale worked on his great translation of the Bible in Cologne, Worms and Antwerp; Wren gained inspiration for St Paul's from study of the Louvre and of the Val de Grace in Paris; Hans Sloane discussed botany with Linnaeus*; William Chambers, the great architect of Hanoverian Britain, was born in Sweden; Hume knew the French philosophes and was the driving impetus who woke Kant 'from his dogmatic slumbers'; Wordsworth travelled in France (as well as Germany) and wrote of his experiences in his remarkable autobiographical poem 'The Prelude'; Byron was the inspiration for the entire European Romantic movement; Shelley set up his bizarre ménage in Switzerland, and Keats wound his way down to Italy where he died, whilst Byron went on to Greece to die; Constable influenced Delacroix who influenced the Impressionists. Alexander von Humboldt's account of his extraordinary journey to Latin America inspired the young Charles Darwin to undertake the voyage of the Beagle. And the impact on George Eliot of Germany (and of the great German modernist biblical scholar D.F.Strauss in particular) is obvious in her work, including her greatest masterpiece, *Middlemarch*. No list

---

* In Latin, because it was the only language they had in common – a late example of Latin's role as Europe's language of intellectual interaction.

of British literary connexions with the Continent would be complete without D.H.Lawrence, who eloped to Germany in 1912 with the German wife of his professor at Nottingham, and later wrote some of his best poetry in Sicily.* And so on as the twentieth century unfolded into its horrors and into an irreversible modernity of spirit. This was the time when T.S.Eliot, the American turned quintessential Englishman who revered Dante, spent a literary career yearning to recover (and ultimately not finding?) a holistic vision for the human spirit as expressed in the European culture he so passionately valued – a vision that would be a faint echo of what Dante had done for the medieval European spirit.

So at every stage of the intellectual life of Europe, people from this country have played leading roles. The historical development of the British identity, with its outward – and eventually imperial – focus, in no way caused the exchange and interplay to slacken. In other words, this European conversation was, and remains, an essential part of the British spirit and of the British identity. We share so much more with the other Europeans than just our geography: there are deep cultural continuities we cannot deny without denying our history and impoverishing ourselves.

---

* Although Frieda and he were not in Germany for long – the outbreak of war saw to that – the influence of Germany remained with Lawrence for life, with an obvious impact in particular in his notorious *Lady Chatterley's Lover*, in which the paralysed Sir Clifford expatiates on the suffering of the enemy in terms which Wilfred Owen would have recognised, and reads aloud to Connie from Rilke and Hauptmann.

This is not to say that British cultural expression is just another European voice without any distinctive accent – any more than French, German, Italian or Spanish voices are just those of a Europe in unison. These voices are all different, all influenced by their language and their history in ways which have created distinct styles and outlooks. No one could mistake the world of Shakespeare for that of Racine or of Cervantes. No one could mistake that unique blend of metaphysics and music which is Germany for anywhere else. Yet the totality is not a series of separate streams that never mingle. Instead they coalesce and separate and come together again as at the delta of a great river where it reaches the sea. And the flow of British spiritual life is one of these intermingling streams.

One thing is clear: for all the differences, Britain has more in common with these neighbours of ours than it does with America. Europeans share much with America, of course. At one level, we are all children of the Enlightenment. We all share the values that are common to democracies – values which are all too often taken for granted by those who have never had to live without them and never had to fight for them. The British share something else too: the origins of the American colonies have left a residual sense that we are cousins, even if Americans who can trace their roots back to those who rebelled against George III are a tiny minority in the modern melting pot. They also share the language, which makes for superficially easy communication.

But at another level there are obvious differences in values and priorities. American ideology is famously individualistic (whilst also being patriotic to a degree which we and other

Europeans find mawkish). It has also had no pre-Enlightenment past to react against (and therefore, ironically, nurtures more pre-Enlightenment thought patterns – notably the widespread pre-scientific attitude towards evolution and human origins). Religion plays a very different role in American life than in a much more thoroughly secularised Europe – more public, more intrinsic to the social structure, more important to the individual's social identity – despite the constitutional separation of church and state. And there are obvious differences between European and American assumptions about, for example, the right way to provide health care in society, or in attitudes to abortion, to capital punishment or to gun control. These are all reminders that the centre of gravity of the American identity is very different from that of Europe. They are a reminder to the British, who are more apt than other Europeans to overlook these differences, that we in fact have far more in common with our continental neighbours and less with our transatlantic friends than we often recognise. The British identity has, after all, a strong European core.

The mirror crack'd?

There is one other question for the British identity at its Brexit crossroads: will it survive intact at all?

Scottish politics have been dominated by the question of independence now for a generation. In the run up to the 2014 referendum, attitude surveys consistently showed that more Scots identified themselves as Scottish than as British. The Scottish establishment may have done well in earlier times out of the British Empire; but Scotland's nineteenth-century experience was of industrialisation and of large-scale Irish immigration creating sectarian tensions that contaminated Scottish urban life until recently. Then came deindustrialisation and the oil boom, which simultaneously fuelled resentment of London and a new dream of an independent future as wealthy as that of Norway. The rise of the Scottish Nationalists and the strength of the pro-European vote draw on the same yearning for a separate and robust identity. Scottish nationalism has one thing in common with Ireland: for both, the European Union offers a context in which to assert and protect their identity (over and against Britain in the case of the Irish, and England in the case of Scottish nationalists). The irony is therefore that, at one level, the case for Scottish independence now has a clearer rationale, because Brexit is a threat to the Scottish identity by denying Scotland that European dimension – and yet the economic and political risk of such a course is now manifestly much greater than in 2014.

At the very least, though, this means that centrifugal tendencies will tug away within the new 'Global Britain' just when it is seeking to assert itself coherently and in a new way on the world stage. And this reminds us, as we fret about a possible breakaway by the Scots, about something else: the United Kingdom has broken up before. The Irish tragedy culminated in a bitter battle for independence, in civil war and in partition, followed in the north by decades of sectarian mistrust and strife, and in the Republic by decades of struggle to realise an identity attuned to the modern world. But that is now past: one of the crowning achievements of the EU has been to enable the Irish to find their identity in the wider context of the new Europe. If ever there was a country whose experience proves the value of the EU as what the former German Chancellor Helmuth Kohl used to call the 'house of Europe', Ireland is it. Its experience through the financial and economic crisis has been far from painless, but at a deep level it has not only modernised and transformed itself, but acquired a new self-esteem and confidence on the international stage. The British no longer tell patronising jokes about the Irish: but during the Brexit campaign, they still treated Ireland as an afterthought. Yet the six million British citizens who are entitled to Irish passports will retain a degree of freedom that the rest of the country has denied itself.

Meanwhile, in the north the spiralling violence was finally stilled by the Good Friday Agreement which planted a new, vulnerable tree of opportunity, constantly in need of protection and nurture, regularly at risk of being uprooted.

Northern Ireland does not have a coherent identity and is very unlikely ever to achieve one: it is, in effect, in a holding pattern. The Brexit vote produced a majority to remain, but unlike in Scotland this majority was not uniform. The nationalist vote was solidly for remaining; the unionist vote was divided. The consequences have yet to be played out: it is possible that recent political developments signal the beginning of some sort of endgame. The question for post-EU Britain is whether it can establish a new settlement that supports, rather than undermines, peace and gradual reconciliation on the island of Ireland.

A mature identity for Global Britain?

In short, there are obvious stresses in the fabric of the British identity: the United Kingdom could well breakup further as a result of Brexit. Its continued integrity cannot be taken for granted. The question is whether the new 'Global Britain' which is emerging as the organising vision for the country – both in domestic social policy and in international strategy – will be robust enough to bear the weight of being a true and full expression of that national identity. The answer is that it will only do so if it comes to maturity. There are all too many examples of national identities that are immature – often evidenced either by an arrogant, unexamined confidence that is oblivious to the reactions of others, or by a brittle assertiveness which betrays low self-esteem just as clearly at the national level as it does in an individual. The British have been guilty of the former in times past: the risk is of falling into the latter trap in this new era.

At home, we have walked by too often on the other side – so often in fact that we have not noticed what was actually there in our midst. And internationally, we have lived with too many unexamined assumptions about the history of our dealings with others. We have not read ourselves in the faces of those others. We live with the consequences still: the concentrated and self-referential establishment in London, and the assumption that we have a special role in the world, given to us by a history which the world ought to admire. Just as we live with what the Brexit vote told us about what we have become, so we live with what it tells us about who we think we are.

This may seem harsh. But there is purpose in this harshness. Achieving maturity in the future will depend on how well we come to terms with the past. In our individual lives we don't hesitate to acknowledge that spiritual maturity comes through honest self-analysis, recognition and renewal. This is true of nations too. Other nations, both in Europe and beyond, have reason enough to acknowledge this truth. But we do too. Brexit is one of the those history-making crossroads which – whatever else it means – gives us occasion for reflection which, if honest, cannot help involving introspection and a renewed commitment to the common good. That is now our challenge. To be honest about our history, to invest in our people, and to be good neighbours in Europe – which means to recognise that, like all neighbours, we are part of the community. And thus to be robust in our identity – an identity that will be both old and new. It will draw both on our ancient European heritage and also on the best instincts of that new British self which came into life in the eighteenth century; and it will learn from the inevitably mixed story of sins and glory which is British history since then. All this is essential if we are to be open to the world – to be the mature global citizen implied by Global Britain.

The European Identity
Historical and Cultural Realities We Cannot Deny
Stephen Green

Is there any such thing as a European identity? Amidst
all the kaleidoscopic variety what – if anything – do
28 members of the European Union have in common?
The facts of history have created shared interests and
cultural connections that are in the end more important
than the differences. We know we are different from
Asia; and we are more different from America than
we – perhaps especially the British – think. So in a 21st
century of globalisation and emerging great powers,
Europe must discover and define that common identity.
This is a challenge for all the big states of the EU.

'[This] little paperback argues for realism about Britain's
options and its connections with the Continent'
Church Times

'a timely contribution'
Centre for Policy Studies

'stimulating and informative reading on
the fate of the European Union'
Strategic Policy

Breaking Point
The UK Referendum on the EU and its Aftermath
Gary Gibbon

Into a year teeming with global volatility, David Cameron
introduced another giant unknown, rolling the dice
on Britain's most important economic relationship: its
43-year-old membership of the EU. In European capitals
this was seen as an existential threat to the entire European
project, while Eurosceptics across the UK saw it as the
perfect moment to pull up the drawbridge. The political
establishment fired back with a barrage of government
data, third-country endorsements and world bodies'
opinions, unsure whether these long-trusted political
weapons weren't firing blanks. *Breaking Point* explains
where post-referendum Britain is heading, how we got
here, and what lessons might be learned. It combines
analysis of official and off-the-record meetings with
senior politicians as well as with ordinary voters.

'an informative mixture of diary and analysis that starkly
lays out the shortcomings of the Remain campaign'
Financial Times

The UK In-Out Referendum
EU Foreign and Defence Policy Reform
David Owen

The EU's attempts at conflict resolution have left much to be desired. In the Ukraine, the Baltic States, Turkey and much of the Middle East, there is a lack of coherent policy. This book argues that the renegotiations around the UK's referendum vote represent an opportunity to enact wide-scale reform, not least to ensure that the nations of an increasingly politically integrated Eurozone do not come to dominate the Foreign and Security policy of the EU in years to come. To allow them to do so would almost certainly see the policy of 'common defence' advance at the expense of the United States' lasting commitment to NATO. Former Foreign Secretary David Owen argues that should Britain's reform negotiations with the EU fail there will be serious implications for our security, and that foreign policy and security belong at the heart of the reforms the EU so desperately needs.

'the ambition of the EU to become a super-state, with its own army backing its own strategic objectives, is a challenge to NATO, not an attempt to strengthen the U.S.-led Western Alliance ... This point is made with great authority'
Dominic Lawson, *Daily Mail*

'At last, a grown-up book about the issue of the moment'
Compulsive Reader

Britain in a Perilous World
The Strategic Defence and Security Review We Need
Jonathan Shaw

In 2010 the coalition government's Strategic Defence and Security Review hit the headlines for all the wrong reasons. Major defence projects such as the NIMROD aircraft were abandoned at huge cost while others were controversially continued because they were too expensive to scrap. Major General Jonathan Shaw argues persuasively for the need to rethink the way Whitehall devises strategy and reaches decisions. Taking the imprecise use of language as his starting point, Shaw challenges the assumptions that underlie Whitehall practice. Based on extensive personal experience of working in Whitehall and applying strategy in the field, Shaw provides a piercing insight into how government really works. In this powerfully argued piece, he suggests how the Review can be improved and why the credibility of our political class depends on getting it right.

'brilliant ... a must-read for any British politician or political journalist'
The Week

'a firecracker ... a must-read for anyone interested in the failings of Whitehall'
Evening Standard